Best wishes from

Paul Jennings

Aylsham August 1986

East Anglia

East Anglia Watercolours

by John Tookey Words by Paul Jennings

Gordon Fraser · London

First published 1986 by
The Gordon Fraser Gallery Ltd, London and Bedford
Copyright   Illustrations: John Tookey, 1986
                    Text: Paul Jennings, 1986

ISBN 0 86092 089 5

Text set by August Filmsetting, Haydock
Origination by Adroit Photo Litho Ltd, Birmingham
Printed by The Roundwood Press Ltd, Kineton, Warwick
Bound by Hunter & Foulis Ltd, Edinburgh
Map drawn by Hanni Bailey
Designed by Peter Guy

Contents

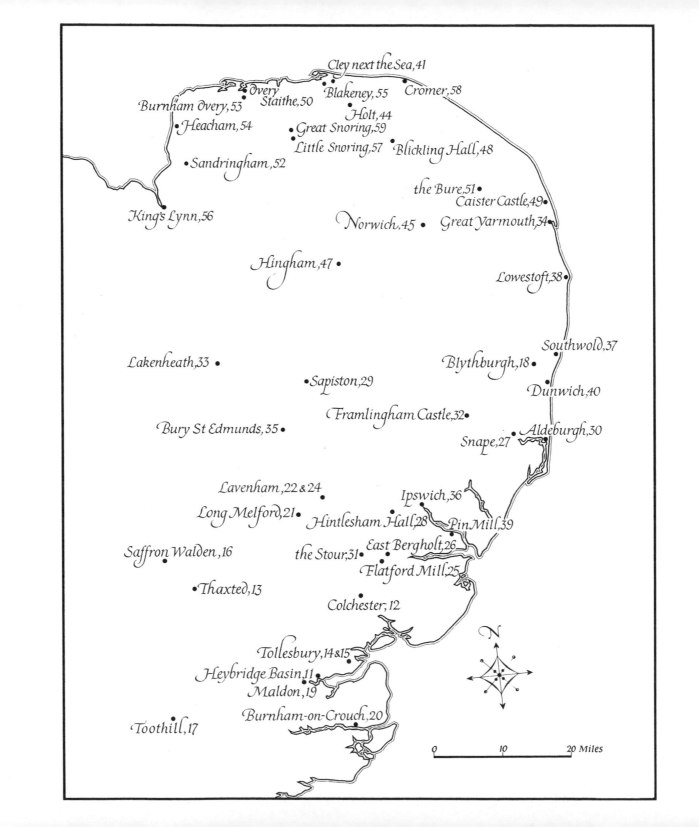

Cley next the Sea, 41

Blakeney, 55   Cromer, 58

Overy
Burnham Overy, 53   Staithe, 50   Holt, 44

• Heacham, 54   Great Snoring, 59

Little Snoring, 57   • Blickling Hall, 48

• Sandringham, 52

the Bure, 51 •

Caister Castle, 49•

King's Lynn, 56 •   Norwich, 45 •   • Great Yarmouth, 34•

Hingham, 47 •

Lowestoft, 38•

Southwold, 37

Lakenheath, 33 •   Blythburgh, 18•

• Sapiston, 29   Dunwich, 40

Framlingham Castle, 32•

Bury St Edmunds, 35 •   • Aldeburgh, 30

Snape, 27

Lavenham, 22 & 24 •

Ipswich, 36•

Long Melford, 21•   Hintlesham Hall, 28   Pin Mill, 39

Saffron Walden, 16 •   East Bergholt, 26

the Stour, 31 •   Flatford Mill, 25

• Thaxted, 13

Colchester, 12

N

Tollesbury, 14 & 15

Heybridge Basin, 11 •

Maldon, 19

• Toothill, 17   Burnham-on-Crouch, 20

0   10   20 Miles

Introduction

If there was some way of getting a hundred artists to paint a picture called simply 'East Anglia' and fusing their efforts into an Identikit whole, it is a fair bet that the result would show some kind of open or slightly rolling landscape, with perhaps willows lining a slow and placid river, a glimpse of the sea— and certainly a church, made of flint, perhaps a noble tower dominating the kind of ridge which hereabouts gives you the feeling of being able to see about twenty miles. The flint in such a picture would have to be painted only one colour unless they could manage an infinitely subtler version of that holograph colour-change thing found on credit cards, which could mirror the infinite changes of this material from silver to beige to grey to ochre to a dazzling yellow or near-white in the ever-changing light of these huge skies.

Of course there are also snug villages and towns whose origins go back to antiquity: Norwich with its cathedral and castle, and at North Elmham the great ruins of a *Saxon* cathedral which is centuries older—not to mention the Christian symbols that were found on some of the famous fourth-century Mildenhall Treasure, dating from when there were still Romans here. We have two places actually called Caister (castrum or camp), one by Norwich and the other by Yarmouth. Admittedly the Romans didn't land here first, but pretty well everyone else did. In Friesland there are villages called Barrum, Blya, Jislum and Nyland; we have Barham, Blyth, Gisleham and Nayland...

Warriors came and turned into farmers, only to face another lot of warriors, races fought and mixed. From all those melting-pot centuries it was Anglia, out of the Heptarchy or Seven Kingdoms of pre-Norman Conquest England (Kent, East Anglia, Sussex, Wessex, Northumbria, Mercia and Essex) that finally gave its name to our country, even though the first nationally recognised King was Egbert of Wessex who reigned from 802 to 836. But before we get on to Constable and the marvellous medieval cloth-making villages and the sailing creeks and the sandy Brecklands and the high boulder-clay wheatlands and the clouds and the light and the marshes and the sheer *otherness* of it all, let us consider the Wuffingas.

This was not an Anglo-Saxon breed of dog, but a dynasty named after Wuffa, a leader of what archaeologists describe as the Ipswich People, the source of the famous seventh-century Treasure of Sutton Hoo, who are known to have shared boat-burial customs with the people of what is now Sweden. Claiming descent from the Caesars (!) the Wuffingas had a descendant called Raedwald who became a Christian in 617 but, as Bede relates, had another altar set up for offerings to devils, just in case; and he was for a time recognised as overlord of all southern England—some say of *all* England. The village of Ufford, just north of Woodbridge, takes its name from Wuffa. There is nothing in the country to match the 1450 font cover, eighteen feet high, in its church.

It all depends what you mean by East Anglia. In the strict Heptarchy sense it meant Suffolk (a name first known in 895), Norfolk (not known as such till 1043), Cambridge and the Isle of Ely. Essex (Land of the East Saxons) didn't come into it. But in modern parlance it does and so it comes into this book, whereas Cambridgeshire (worth a book on its own, with everything from King's or Trinity or Ely to the wild lonely Fens) doesn't. In other words, this book covers the three counties which have a coastline.

This brings us to the heart of the lovely paradox of East Anglia (however you choose to define it) which its geography and history have combined to produce. The very creeks and inlets and estuaries which brought the invaders meant that there could never be a ribbon-development coast road today. It is true that once you get as far up as Lowestoft you can drive right round to Hunstanton and never be more than a mile or so from the sea; but quite often you will be going through a wood or a wheatfield or a snug inland village; sometimes you *will* touch the sea, sometimes you will get a distant view of it over marshes.

Above all, the moment you stop and talk to any true East Anglian you will realise how fortunate this area was to escape the full horrors of the Industrial Revolution. Forget for a moment that today Felixstowe is the biggest container port in the country, that North Sea gas comes ashore hereabouts, and that there are tank farms and silos and coachbuilding and goodness

knows what else in King's Lynn. You are in an area where the rivers did not flow fast enough to power the new machinery, though for centuries they carried the wool and cloth which played a major part in funding the unequalled number of churches and timber-framed houses. So for two or three centuries this land was quite content to be England's almost forgotten agricultural backwater (even though in Coke of Holkham and 'Turnip' Townshend of Raynham, Norfolk produced the two men who revolutionised farming).

Strangers are often surprised by the appearance of huge churches practically in the middle of nowhere; but this is because several parishes would often share a church, and each 'hundred' had its minster or monastery. Similarly, there are (in Suffolk, for instance) almost as many isolated, usually moated farmhouses as there are medieval churches (about 500), because estates could be parcelled up and sold separately after being left to several sons. This system was called 'partible inheritance' and was pretty unusual in medieval times. More yeomen than lords around here.

The result was a close-knit community marvellously spread over open land. It is impossible to say, now that everyone watches the same television, whether the unbridgeable gulf between the slow-sharp, secret-sharing natives and the ever-growing number of immigrants, so fully detailed in Ronald Blythe's *Akenfield*, is or will remain unbridgeable for ever. What is certain is that centuries of being on the way to nowhere but itself *have* produced a marvellous race of people whose characteristic way of addressing each other as 'bor'— short for 'neighbour'—reflects their homogeneity. Everyone by now knows the kind of joke produced by their long familiarity with the earth, the seasons, nature in life and death. Indeed, there are books of such jokes. Old lady goes into Bonds', the big Norwich department store.

'Oi want a mournin' hat. It's me husband.'
'Oh', says the shop assistant, 'I'm sorry to hear you have lost him.'
'Oh, that ain't gone yit, but Oi can only get in hare Sat'dys.'

You don't need to buy such books if you live here, as I have had the unending pleasure of doing for thirty years—so anyway four of our six children *are* Suffolk natives. The wonderful district nurse who delivered them all (at home) told us of an old shepherd and his wife whom she used to visit about twice a week. One morning, quite early, not long after eight a.m., she called in since she was passing. There was the old man, fully dressed, having a cup of tea. The nurse asked him where his wife was.

'That's gorn', he said.
'What do you mean? Gone out?'
'No, no. That died. In the night.'
'Goodness! What did you do?'
'Well, I saw I couldn't do nawthen for the pore ole gal. So I slept along of her till it wor light. That didn't disturb me much.'

The other thing to remember about East Anglia is that it is always much bigger than you think. Once a composer friend of ours was having a work performed at the Norwich Festival (one of the oldest in the country), so I suggested a kind of high tea, then off we would go, from East Bergholt where we then lived. It was approaching six p.m., and we were gobbling while he seemed very inclined to take his time (the concert was at eight). At last I had to ask him to hurry. 'Why?' he said. 'It's only just down the road, isn't it?' After a hair-raising dash along that A140, in a thunderstorm, we made it by about two minutes.

And as you will deduce, if only from this book, there is a great deal more of it *after* Norwich. Perhaps it will all get to look and be much the same as the rest of England in the end. But it will need at least another thousand years to do so. Meanwhile, you could spend your whole life exploring East Anglia for new and secret marvels (and an old, familiar marvel —say Blythburgh Church—can turn into a new one when floodlit or caught in a sudden April sunshine). This book presents an artist's impressions, not the usual coloured photographs; here and there a roof line may have been altered, a pub sign or tree moved—though all the facts in it are (it is hoped) just facts.

East Anglia has always inspired both the artist and the ordinary visitor. We hope to inspire you before you start your visit, help you whilst making it, and remind you after you return. If you live here already may we dare to hope it will bring a fresh reminder that you are jolly lucky.

Heybridge Basin

There is only one road to the Heybridge Basin which runs east of the spit of land separating it from Maldon. The River Blackwater here is aptly called Colliers Reach and there is a lock into the canal to Chelmsford which received Parliamentary assent in 1793, after 120 years of opposition from Maldon, which thought, no doubt with justification, that it would take some of its trade. You come through a jumble of houses, some of them old traditional weatherboard cottages, some perfectly ordinary semis, with masts visible over their low roofs. Walk down to the river: the Jolly Sailor pub, a huge vista of water, the trees of Northey and Osea Islands and distant sails again beyond. Turn right (i.e. westward) on the riverbank: there is the canal lock, and the Old Ship pub at the end of an enchanting row of *ultra*-traditional cottages lining the Basin's end. ('Cor, like the M1, isn't it!' said a passer-by surveying the three-abreast fishing-boats, an abandoned-looking Thames barge with thistles and grass on the gunwhales, and smart boats with names like *Love in a Mist*). But there are strong remnants of the old-established, independent, pub-based community. A local boat was seen bringing parts from HMS *Belfast* (in the Thames) for repair here and the revived regatta includes pole-vaulting over the lock.

Colchester

Like many old towns nowadays (and they don't come any older than Colchester, scene of Boadicea's short-lived triumph over the Romans in 61 A.D.), this one has a central commercial citadel, with a High Street, the usual chain stores and a pleasant new pedestrian shopping precinct, surrounded by a one-way system almost as defensive as medieval walls. But here you can walk back centuries, sometimes millennia, in a hundred yards. From the broad, market-holding High Street, just past the Town Hall (from its top native St Helena, discoverer of the True Cross, faces Jerusalem) this street goes down to the 'Dutch Quarter', illustrating *inter alia* Colchester's extraordinary richness in doors and fanlights. Further down is the largest Norman keep in Europe, crammed with Roman-till-recent exhibits. Elsewhere are the noble Norman ruined nave of St Botolph's Priory and the gatehouse to St John's, the first Augustinian abbey in England. And don't miss the delightful Mercury Theatre, one of the pioneers of provincial theatre renaissance.

Thaxted

Thaxted is a smaller, neater, convex version of Saffron Walden. Although the latter town is concave, in a valley, the spire of its church does dominate even when you approach, as you must, from above. But it obviously cannot dominate as does the magnificent 181-foot spire of Thaxted's noble church, queen of these rich boulder-clay uplands, looking down also on an enchanting medieval townlet with occasional eighteenth-century overlays. The main street curves gently down in greys, blues, pastel yellows, to what at the bottom must stir the heart of any music-lover; the house, marked by a blue plaque, where Holst lived from 1917 to 1925. He first moved, in 1914, to a cottage (since burnt) at the higher end. It was here, in the pre-motorised silence of those days, before Thaxted could be easily reached from the M11 let alone look like being under threat from the flight-path of an extended Stansted Airport, that the extraordinary mystical harmonies of the *Planets* suite grew in his mind. From the nearby Guildhall, showing a greater 'wealth of exposed beams' than when the cutlers (the town's major Tudor industry) built it, two wonderful streets lead back up to the church now forever associated with Holst and the famous socialist Christian vicar Conrad Noel. Both believed that heaven was singing and dancing, and vice versa.

Tollesbury, low water

Anyone wishing to explore the wide-skied, water-and-wheatlands north shore of the Blackwater estuary (Tollesbury is the last, or first, village there) and the surprising, comfortable, been-here-for-ages hamlets which suddenly appear among lonely marshes and creeks, should come from Colchester, Britain's oldest city and, in the time of the Emperor Claudius (43 A.D.), its first capital. It is pleasant to leave Colchester by an unexpectedly bosky bit of the B1018, and emerge on to wide vistas of distant water and cornlands of the London clay (but for a few millennial geological accidents the Thames itself might have come up here), in which ochre-ish rubbly stone, *septaria*, is also found. It is in the eleventh-century base of the church's great four-square tower. Many periods are reflected including the font bought from a 1718 fine on a man who 'came drunk into ye Church and cursed and talked aloud', and a modern window, presented by a New Yorker, which shows great J—class yachts, skippered in the America's Cup by local men. Then down vague road to these busy solitudes of waterside.

Tollesbury, boatyard

Saffron Walden

The wonderful thing is that Saffron Walden is all that you would expect from what is surely one of the most romantically euphonious place-names in England, which is saying something. Odd to think its etymology is *wealh denu*, 'the valley of the serfs' (ie Britons, ie, to the Saxon invaders, the We(a)lsh). Saffron Wal(es)den. The saffron part comes from the autumn crocus: 30,000 were needed to make 1 lb of the dye used on medieval cloth. It grew prolifically on clay-cum-chalk—from central Essex boulder-clay to the great chalk uplands. A magnificent Perpendicular church (with a splendid organ), airy and light, above a medieval grid with little passages ('twitchells'), demonstrates the town's Tudor prosperity later harmoniously mingled with Georgian and Victorian (for example the Market Place, with a central fountain by John Bentley, architect of Westminster Cathedral). But escape the roaring High Street traffic and explore on foot.

Toothill

The late Sir John Betjeman, lecturing to the Friends of Essex Churches, said 'I always feel I *am* in Essex long before I am out of north-east London ... and not only because of the colour of the bricks'. Certainly you can leave London some way west of the A12 and feel, instantly, the *forest* element of this southernmost part of East Anglia. Epping was one of six 'royal forests', and Forest Law covered not only thickly wooded areas but the kind of view-halloo landscape, today heath-cum-wheatland, where you may find down some hidden lane groups of farm buildings such as these near Toothill. Here you are not only south of the end of the London Underground at Ongar and the Government-secret-looking forest of aerials at North Weald; you are well under twenty miles from Central London. You are also about three minutes' drive from a church which has no lack of friends, being the famous Greensted-juxta-Ongar, the oldest wooden church in the world, the black oak walls dating from 850; a secret, quiet, tree-surrounded little miracle.

Blythburgh

You are looking south, from a lay-by on the A12 road from Great Yarmouth. The building on the left is a concrete water-tower built in 1953. A yard behind you there is a roar of traffic as the impatient queue behind some juggernaut waits for the next straight bit—then all is reed-whistling, bird-calling peace as you gaze across at Holy Trinity, 'the Cathedral of the Marshes', one of the great glories of Suffolk, indeed of East Anglia—then the next traffic comes. But turn off the main road to the sudden and permanent quiet of the church and it will really take your breath away. The south nave parapet presents a wonderful stone lacework of exuberant quatrefoil over most of its amazing 127-foot length. In the flint tower are great blue stones, black ones, bits of brick; you look up at it and down over the marshes and meadows.

But inside, ah, inside, what wide white brick-floored clear-glass *space*, accentuated by quiet Blythburgh's tumultuous history: the seventh-century King Anna, father of St Etheldreda (a pre-Reformation dedicatee of Ely cathedral), the rise and decline of Blythburgh port, the Priory (now ruined), fifteenth-century rebuilding, appalling hacking by the Puritan iconoclast Dowsing, semi-dereliction (an early nineteenth-century congregation needed umbrellas *inside*) and the total destruction overhead in 1944 of US bomber with Joseph Kennedy, eldest son, aboard. The angel roof has been restored; some come to see this, some to see the famous bench-ends (Seven Deadly Sins etc.) but most come for the whole inspired and inspiring thing.

Maldon is particularly famous for three things: the battle against the Vikings lost by Byrhtnoth in the tenth century and the epic poem about it; sea-salt; and—but it is best to come on the third by surprise. Starting from the posh end (the best hotel, solicitors'-offices end), walk down the High Street, past All Saints church (with the horse trough outside on which it simply says 'To the memory of a good mother who lived in this town'), past the unexpected library (with the *very* old brown books amassed by Dr Plume) joined onto the thirteenth-century tower of St Peter's church since the nave collapsed in 1665. Continue past increasingly DIY etc. shops, disused cinema, and Chinese restaurants, then fork left down Church Street—and, in the last few yards, a sudden miracle. With yet another magnificent squat-towered church, St Mary the Virgin, on your right, you drop down to the waterfront, the Hythe. Chartering has brought new life to the barges, and these three freshly-painted ones prove it. They have no keel (shallow waters here), a huge 'lee-board' is lowered from the side when going about. There were 2,000 of them in 1900. Now chartering, private or trust ownership, and the Maldon, Pin Mill and other races are just in time to save a precious few.

Maldon

Burnham-on-Crouch

Burnham-on-Crouch is really the extreme south-eastern limit of the great east coast estuarine sailing complex. No doubt a few people keep boats on the only river to the south of it before you come to the Thames itself—the Roach, which divides northwards into the Crouch and southwards, round the island of Foulness, with its mysterious Ministry of Defence DANGER warnings in red ink on the Ordance maps. Perhaps they even keep them in such North Thames resorts as Southend-on-Sea. But that is a London suburb compared with Burnham, 'the Cowes of the East Coast', still pure weatherboard Essex and completely dominated by sailing. The Royal Burnham Yacht Club mounted Britain's challenge for the America's Cup in 1983. Its chandlers stock books with titles like *This is Racing* and *This is Rough-Weather Cruising*. A walk along its river front shows you boats moored as far as you can see in both directions, except when some huge ship-builder's shed intervenes. And on the other side delightful, infinitely varied domestic architecture, intimate private gardens, places selling cream teas—and more shipwrights.

Long Melford

Unless you count Sudbury (now practically contiguous), the aptly-named Long Melford is the largest place you pass through on what used to be a favoured way from Colchester and north Essex to Cambridge and the Midlands (now, thank goodness, catered for by the semi-motorway A45). There is therefore less traffic on the road following the Stour Valley through a chain of magical villages—Stoke-by-Nayland, the town of Sudbury (Gainsborough's home), Long Melford, Cavendish (marvellously re-thatched cottages on green), Clare (with its great Augustinian priory), and Stoke-by-Clare. You climb slightly from this broad street where Tudor, Georgian and modern houses are harmoniously conjoined (and words like *ristorante* are beginning to appear), to a superb triangular village green, Melford Hall (an Elizabethan masterpiece: mellow brick, pepperpot towers etc.) and one of the finest Perpendicular churches in Suffolk (and therefore in the world). If you see nothing else see its quiet, almost detached Lady Chapel and its Lily Crucifixion window. It is—well, the Crucifixion and lilies. Unique.

Lavenham High Street

You may find youself walking down Lavenham High Street behind anything from a youth group to a couple of experts trying to decide whether a timber-framed house is of the (obviously rare here) 'Wealden' type (cross-wings at either end and small hall between them all under one long roof) or an ordinary 'hall-house' (cross-wings under own independent gable). Or a family group simply taking in the beauty of it all. But the main impression *is* of timber frame—whether still properly plastered over as some of it was meant to be, with some beams properly exposed as they were meant to be, or wrongly exposed when antiquarian enthusiasm at the start of this century assumed they *all* had to be exposed. You will also notice such signs as 'Hair Stylist' and 'Diners Club' and a well-painted prosperous air to which mobility of new residents, retirement buying, and indeed tourism have all contributed. Yet in 1912 someone bought the Wool Hall, no less, and dismantled this great medieval pre-fab. It was bought straight back and re-installed only because of the preservation-minded Princess Louise. As late as 1949 the *Sunday Chronicle* captioned a photograph of decaying houses 'Picture Postcard Town is Slum'. Not any more.

Suffolk poppies

Lavenham, Market Place

The glorious tower of the famous church of Sts Peter and Paul stands four-square at the north-west corner and boundary of England's best-preserved Tudor town. It looks down on fields, and can be seen from miles away, (like Kersey, Stoke-by-Nayland and many another of Suffolk's ridge-dominating towers). In fact you can stand in the ancient centre of Lavenham's life, its market place, (at the opposite corner from the church), and see fields, past medieval streets, in any direction. But the real way to take Lavenham is by surprise, coming on it suddenly through Monks Eleigh and Brent Eleigh, along the secret bed of a River Brett tributary, to be delighted (it was so in 1985 anyway) by the rare sight of hedges being planted, instead of grubbed up, and long-stemmed corn (thatch as well as bread, maybe?) piled in those almost-forgotten stooks. Then, where to start? You can't miss the Guildhall; you can't miss Little Hall, now, appropriately, HQ of the Suffolk Preservation Society but once the home of the Gayer-Andersons who founded the equally beautiful 'Cretan Woman's House' museum in Cairo. And you can't *possibly* miss Shilling Street.

Flatford Mill

Anyone native-looking in Bergholt (a village not devoid of good things) is liable to be asked from a car 'Where is Flatford Mill?'. It, and the neighbouring Willy Lott's cottage (behind your left shoulder as you look at this picture), are, after Anne Hathaway's, surely the best-known in the world. (A local lad, noticing a fly-blown *Hay Wain* in one of those last-gas-for-200-miles places in Arizona, was not allowed to pay for anything when they finally believed that he lived in sight of it.) But it is hidden, a mile down from Bergholt—you can only do the last few yards on foot. Then walk a mere 200 yards along the meadow-marsh path and you can see, far off, the main London-Yarmouth line. But you can't see Flatford from the train, or anywhere else. Hidden, among cows, willows, meadows, skies, poplars, with distant sights of Dedham and Stratford St Mary churches. Hidden; the place where Constable made local and particular sights into universal and noble art.

'I am come to a determination to make no idle visits this summer, nor to give up my time to commonplace people. I shall return to Bergholt . . .' wrote Constable in 1802 to his friend John Dunthorne, village plumber, amateur artist and perhaps first teacher. Constable, 'the handsome miller', born 1776, had only three years previously got his miller father's reluctant consent to become a student at the Royal Academy. He is still the presiding genius of this hitherto obscure village. Its church, uniquely, has its five great bells in a wooden cage adjoining it, the tower never having been finished. They are parked upside down, on great axles, with counterweights, and are rung by hand. Constable's marvellously happy marriage with the grand-daughter of the rector, Dr Rhudde, was preceded by a long courtship because of the old man's disdain for a mere painter. Dunthorne's house was on the left of this (not literal) view. Out of sight in a little road to the right of the petrol pump is the tiny house Constable used as a studio when he returned to East Bergholt.

East Bergholt

Snape

In a shop here, with a heady, high-class holiday-gift aroma compounded of strawberry and other pot-pourris, beeswax, wine and barbecue spices, and wood and straw things, you may buy a booklet about Snape. It contains nineteenth-century photographs of beard-ed labourers with the malt shovels they plied in the hot, humid, long buildings, one of which was transformed into surely the most romantic 800-seat concert hall in the world (it is behind the trees). What would those same labourers have made of the elegant audiences who spill out in the intervals of concerts by world-famous musicians to gaze, past Henry Moore and Barbara Hepworth bronzes (hers two magic totem poles which are also sort of persons made of giant TV sets and holes, through which lightly tanned holiday children shout at each other), over vast reed-beds and waterscapes, to the wooded horizon between them and the sea? Life didn't start here with the Britten-Pears School for Advanced Music Studies. In pre-railway times schooners left for London every Wednes-day from this first (or last) bridge over the River Alde (which refuses to enter the sea at Aldeburgh and turns south, as the Ore, for another eleven miles). And so, too, did brown-sailed Essex barges (top-sail on the seventy-five-foot mast catching winds no one else knew about) loaded with ninety-ton cargoes of barley or hay.

Hintlesham Hall

You have only to walk down the main street of almost any Suffolk village to see a Georgian façade, perhaps with an elegant door and fanlight, on the front of an obviously earlier, timber-framed house. Here you see the same process on a grander, classical scale. Hintlesham Hall began as a Tudor House, the Palladian façade being added in the early eighteenth century. It has known many vicissitudes since the days of its builders, the Timperley family; recusants and, later, Jacobites, who must have been pretty prosperous—you needed to be to pay the fines, let alone build a place like this. Many people came to know it first in the time of its recent owner Anthony Stokes, ex-engineer, amateur handbell-player, organiser of a marvellously curate's-egg, half homely and half

professional, annual Festival. There were Monteverdi operas on an alfresco stage, an orchestra in an empty plunge-bath, and lectures or recitals which were often punctuated by his all too audible conversations on the telephone. After his death the house was beautifully restored by Robert Carrier who made it, not surprisingly, into Suffolk's best-known gourmet restaurant. What would happen to that tradition, people wondered, when he departed for Tangier? It is more than maintained by David and Ruth Watson, who also made it partly residential, with bedrooms overlooking the kind of parkland that makes it impossible to believe you are five miles from Ipswich.

Sapiston

To drive from the Lavenham area (preferably by the narrowest and most circuitous roads you can find), to Sapiston, is to cross the western end of the belt of rich, heavy, clay cornland (Boulder Clay, studded by Ice Age glaciers with flints) of Central or 'High' Suffolk, which runs to the edge of the sandy Brecklands in the county's north-west. You are rarely as high as 200 feet above sea level, but what views—whether under lazy cumulo-nimbus in vast skies over golden standing crops, or with winter bareness making the villages even more obviously well-sited and snug!

And not only villages. There are pretty well the same number of moated farmhouses (around 500) in Suffolk as there are medieval churches. (One of Constable's most famous paintings, in the Victoria and Albert Museum, is *Cottage in a Cornfield*.) The historical reasons for this go back a long way. At the time of Domesday Suffolk had nearly 7,500 'freedmen' —more than the rest of England put together. Drainage-and-defence moats, and 'partible inheritance' which allowed farms to be split up among sons, and therefore the sale of small bits of land unusual for those days, all con-tributed to this.

These cottages are two miles from Sapiston's church which is rescued from total redundancy by about ten services a year. There are tumbled gravestones (though the grass is carefully scythed) surrounded by lonely semi-heath, maize and wheatfields. Inside, pure white peace. No aisles, just pews, and an ancient font (with a canal-boat-type water ewer). Utter silence, except when aircraft from neighbour-ing RAF Honington scream over. Honington was the birthplace of Robert Bloomfield, author of *the* Suffolk poem *The Farmer's Boy*, who worked on a farm at Sapiston.

Aldeburgh

It is hard to say whether the correspondence between the music of Britten, which made Aldeburgh newly famous, and the pure, bleached clarity of this utterly unspoiled Suffolk sea-town, is magical or just obvious, natural and predictable. Just as the romantic, soft-loud, poetic-dramatic, differently-repeated *motifs* of Elgar reflect the orcharded, vague, romantically blurred Welsh-border lands of his youth, so, surely, does the crystalline, taut inventiveness of Britten reflect this land of flint churches which change colour with every passing cloud. Why *newly* famous? Because the poet Crabbe, that marvellous observer, ('. . . when the cattle as they grazing stand/Seem nobler objects than when viewed

from land') was born here. And Aldeburgh's Garrett-Anderson clan produced the Snape Maltings, the famous Leiston works (the Long Shop is now a landmark in industrial archaeology) and England's first woman doctor. Like Burnham, Aldeburgh has a promenade along which you can only walk; then a back street (with the deeply unremarkable Victorian Jubilee Hall, scene of the première of Britten's *Midsummer Night's Dream* and many others); *then* the smartish High Street, with Tudor cinema and intensive, hollyhocked bijou gardens. This look-out tower belonged to the Down-towners, rivals of the Up-towners for spoils from wrecks in sterner, pre-RNLI times.

The Stour

Framlingham Castle

You might almost be forgiven, looking down sixty or seventy feet from the railed walk right round the top of the curtain wall of this great castle, first at the vast, smooth-grassed and now emptied moat, then at the little town alive with the sound of lawn-mowers, then out over the rich surrounding land, for thinking that the place-name was a misprint for 'Farmlingham'. The first castle on this commanding site may have been built by the Raedwald who in 600 was King of East Anglia, per-haps of all England. It was built, destroyed and rebuilt again by the powerful Bigod barons, Dukes of Framlingham almost more than of Norfolk, in endless quarrels with kings from Henry II to John. Later this senior dukedom passed to the Howards, whose glorious family tombs, especially the Gothic-Renaissance-Romanesque one of the third Duke are, with the fine English organ, the chief glories of the noble church above the delicious triangular market place.

Lakenheath

There could not be a better place than East Anglia to illustrate the miraculous, frightening speed with which aviation has developed— primarily, it must be admitted, under the spur of military necessity. The radar which did much to save these islands was born from experiments on Orfordness in 1935. In the days when Britain was 'the unsinkable aircraft carrier' physical nearness still counted. Many a half-crippled Allied bomber landed thankfully, with its last gallon of fuel, at one of the *ninety* airfields in the three counties alone covered by this book. The wind whistles through many a deserted hangar. You may sometimes see a grey-haired British or American ex-airman stop his car and stare silently at the weeds growing through a cracked runway in some lonely wheatfield. Today, US and British jets scream across, leaving a silence as sudden as the noise, and unthinkable missiles can be launched from anywhere—submarines, trucks in remote forests. Airfields with wicked-looking up-to-the-minute planes such as this at Lakenheath (USAAF) are at once more secret and more noisy. All the same, Lakenheath church has 'the best thirteenth-century font in Suffolk' (Norman Scarfe), and neighbouring Mildenhall (also a US airfield) a superb angel roof. Angels....

Great Yarmouth, the quay

There is a decisiveness, a finality about Yarmouth even though it cannot deny the claim of its southern neighbour Lowestoft to be the easternmost point of England. Only Cromer comes next (and *that* is where the coast has already turned westwards to the Wash, and it would not claim to be a big-boat place, more of a resort). It is not called *Great* Yarmouth for nothing. Just above it is Breydon Water, the largest stretch in the meandering Broads system, joined at its seaward end by that system's central river, the Bure, (coming down from the northwest) and at its inland end by the wandering Waveney. Then, as the River Yare, the water behaves exactly like the Alde at Aldeburgh, and turns south. The Yare has one of the longest riverside docks in Europe;

on one fortunate day, the famous replica *Golden Hinde* moored opposite a perfectly magnificent Dutch schooner. Crammed between the river and the sea, before they join at Gorleston, is the entire old city of Yarmouth. There is still quite a lot left, after the wartime air raids, of the medieval Rows and later merchants' houses. The market place (especially on Wednesdays and Fridays), bursts with life and incredible numbers of people eating chips. Then modest, sometimes Regency-looking streets quickly give way to 'Britain's Greatest Holiday Resort': Joyland, Marina Leisure Centre, floral anchors, pony-chaise rides, and two pier theatres with national (i.e. TV) stars. It is Blackpool in reverse; deck-chair thousands face away from the sea towards the afternoon sun.

Bury could be said not only to contain a history of English architecture but to stand for a scale model of the entire country's history. The remains of the body of St Edmund, who was martyred by the Danes in 869 (in the local dialect account of his refusal to apostatise he says to them 'I ain't a goin to give up nuthen fer yew, yew're a rotten lot o' barstids, the whull bloody bag of ye') made its great Benedictine abbey church (fifty feet longer than Norwich Cathedral) England's most famous shrine long before Canterbury. Two late medieval churches still stand in its precincts: St James, hard by the great Norman tower facing Churchgate Street and, facing Tudor and much Georgian elegance, the cathedral of today. It is about a quarter of the size of the one on this site in which, in 1214, the barons swore on the high altar to wrest power from King John, which resulted in the Magna Carta the following year. There are park-type flowers and neat gravel paths among the remains of rubble walls. This was just the Abbot's garden. Two great gateways remain among the tumuli; also a west front so massive that eighteenth-century houses were built into it. The Adam Town Hall must be seen, and the enchanting, restored little Theatre Royal, the Assembly Rooms, the Angel Hotel, and much else.

Bury St Edmunds

Ipswich, Christchurch Mansion

Ipswich, founded by the Anglo-Saxons in the seventh century, has a curious way of making you wonder whether things just happen to it or whether it makes things happen. This beautiful E-shaped Elizabethan house (Dutch gables added later), is right in the town centre, at the bottom corner of a beautiful park (with a great arboretum at the opposite corner). It became the museum only because, in 1894, a local MP persuaded the Corporation to buy it instead of filling it all in with houses. The result is a museum crammed with domestic interest—some fascinating Constables, of early, quasi-photographic exactness, before he developed his famous atmospheric style, some Gainsboroughs, and

more besides. Some plans failed—Cardinal Wolsey's great projected college (only the gateway remains), a scheme making the Gipping navigable to Stowmarket was finished just in time to be upstaged by the new railway. Above all it always has been and still is a port, with all the bustle and visual interest that means. 'One of the most agreeable places in England ... an airy, clean and well-governed town,' wrote Defoe. The other famous writer attracted was, of course, Dickens. You can still drink or stay at the Great White Horse where Mr Pickwick's nocturnal search for his watch had such embarrassing consequences.

Southwold

Southwold is a classic example of a Suffolk coastal town. It is completely unspoilt because only one road, between two lots of water (the Blyth, with glorious Blythburgh church dominating its inland marshes, and the Buss Creek) leads to it. It is like driving on to an island—complete with a dazzling white lighthouse, standing comfortably in a residential road just like any pub or shop. It would be possible for a really lazy motorist to turn left, at the north side of the town, park by the embryonic pier, and not even know about the calm gem of a town up the slight hill. It is all unexpected triangular or oblong greens, from the tiny one near the church, with a companionable seat going all round its huge central wychwood elm, to Tibby's Green or the great vistas of Southwold Common. Or the Town Marshes, bordered by perfect early Victorian or Georgian houses, as though the best bits of Tunbridge Wells had been dropped there overnight. The sandy beaches remember the days of medieval fishing prosperity; the bloody naval Battle of Sole Bay and victory over the Dutch in 1672, whose style is nonetheless everywhere. It is even noticeable in the roofs of the new bungalows by the magnificent church—where the feathered angels and symbol-carrying Apostles and Prophets on its famous screen have only their faces vandalised by the Puritans ('we brake down 130 superstitious pictures . . . and 14 cherubims'). How nice, in this gentle quiet courteous town to see that the great-uncle of a present-day inhabitant carved and painted jolly kings' heads and those of local worthies on the pilasters of Victorian St Edmund's Terrace. And that Adnams, who made England's best beer before the Real Ale Campaign was heard of, use horse drays for local delivery—not sentimentally, but because lorries would be £1,000 a year more expensive.

Lowestoft

For a place so utterly identified with sailing (a sailing club, a waiting list for other moorings, the annual race of the remaining Thames barges with their huge Dutch-painting brown sails, and the locale of Arthur Ransome stories such as *We Didn't Mean To Go To Sea*) Pin Mill is very receptive of non-(or just envious would-be) sailors. The seventeenth-century pub, the Butt and Oyster, overlooking the estuary vista at the bottom of a narrow lane, has wonderful Edwardian advertisements ('Ogden's Gold Cut Cigarettes, 10 for 3d, beware of imitations'; 'Catchpole's Mineral Waters' showing chap in cap chatting up girl in cloche hat in 1930 open car), and a cheerful, unbuttoned air. It is also at the end of a seaward walk along the bank. Under high whispering trees you pass the moored remains of Thames barges which will never sail again, radio and domestic sounds coming from some of them. Then water, white sails, and, suddenly, a large cargo vessel which has come from Ipswich under the huge new bridge to Felixstowe. You're in the rural heart of EEC port country.

Pin Mill

Dunwich

No rays from the holy heaven come down
On the long night-time of that town;
But light from out the lurid sea
Streams up the turrets silently,
Gleams up the pinnacles far and free....

wrote Poe, though his *City in the Sea* was not Dunwich, where aqualung divers can see nothing in the sand-stirred sea which caused this place— thought to have been the base for the mission of St Felix in the seventh century, known to have been a bishopric from 673 to 870—to be literally swallowed up. Already a market town by Domesday, it once rivalled Ipswich as a port and had nine churches (a 'city of chilblained monks'). The worst day was 14 January 1328, when the old harbour was completely choked with shingle. By 1350 over 400 houses had gone. The last medieval church, All Saints, disappeared in this century. Now you can walk up the soft dangerous cliffs beyond these boats, survey the beautiful sweep of the bay from Southwold's elegant light-house to the north and the squat cube of Sizewell nuclear power station to the south and imagine drowned bells. You are on what were the western, *inland* ramparts of the vanished town. Down there, the beautiful huge marsh-view car park, ice cream, fish from fishermen. Up there, the ruined gateway and small remnants of Greyfriars (on Minsmere Road); all that is left.

Cley next the Sea

Cley next the Sea is just that; about a mile from the sea but on the River Glaven, which was once navigable as far as Glandford, about two miles south. It is hereabouts that the Glaven (see Blakeney Marshes) turns westwards. The splendid eighteenth-century Customs House at Cley (pronounced Cly) is evidence of how long this place took to decline, (partly through silting-up and partly through land reclamation after the Enclosures of the early nineteenth century) from its medieval importance as a principal exporter of wool from Norfolk to the Continent. Its huge-naved church, dedicated to St Margaret of Antioch, a splendour even for Norfolk, is evidence of how Cley once made a great statement of civilised human life right on the edge of this wild and desolate coast. How rewarding to walk down the little lane, bordered on both sides by tall hollyhocks (how they seem to thrive in sea air, or is it just the sand?) that leads to this mill (built in 1713) and find that you can explore it. There is a circular sitting-room on the ground floor and on the highest residential floor, fitted carpet corridors lead out to a walkway right round the outside, with incredible views of Blakeney Marshes (and there's a telescope in one of the next rooms up). Then up vertical ladders, to wind-thrumming top chambers with great old cog-wheels and axles lying about. Out-buildings, once stables etc., are now self-catering flats with old Norfolk bird names; *Yarwelp* (Bittern), *Clinker* (Avocet) and, mysteriously, *Silerella* (Bearded Tit).

A Norfolk windmill

A Norfolk mustard field

It seems very appropriate that the building you see across this field of mustard, flowering in its full glory in June in one of the many Norfolk farms under contract to Colman's of Norwich, has the historical-cum-functional appearance of something that could be a fairly modern silo, a medieval dovecote, even a strong-point in a Roman (or Chinese) Wall. Mustard was known (say Colman's) in 3000 B.C. in India, and to everybody from Pythagoras onwards. In the famous parable in St Matthew (Authorised Version, for the sheer joy of it) 'The kingdom of heaven is like to a mustard seed, which man took... which indeed is the least of all seeds: but when it is grown, it is the greatest among herbs, and becometh a tree, so that the birds of the air come and lodge in the branches thereof.' John Eadie's *Biblical Cyclopaedia* (1879) says, endearingly, 'Captains Irby and Mangles think that a species of tree they met with on a journey to Kerek from the southern border of the Dead Sea is the one....' In Norfolk it may not be a tree, but it grows to a man's height, and is thus distinguishable from the other crop which dots *all* England with bright yellow patches earlier in the year, but which is only two feet high: rape.

Holt

The only trouble about motoring through Norfolk is that however slowly you go (and even in Norfolk other drivers get impatient if you hesitate) marvels flash by you. Scarcely are you out of Cley on the road to Holt when you pass a lovely village green on your right; and can you have seen out of the corner of your eye a road called Old Woman's Lane? (Yes.) Then a perfectly *magnificent* green at Wiveton, (pronounced Wivverton) with an equally magnificent church; but can't stop, must get along this beautiful bosky road to Holt. This is practically the perfect Georgian small town, as it was almost entirely rebuilt after a disastrous fire in 1708. At one end of its main street, looking down from Letheringsett Hill, is a milestone-cum-obelisk about ten feet high, with a stone pineapple on top and relevant place-names elegantly incised on each side. About half-way down, after exploring little nooks which you may think are only for pedestrians until something comes nudging gently along, you come to this bit: Fish Hill. But the building on the left is the Leicester Building Society, the one with the Georgian windows is a steak house, next door is an antiquarian bookshop. In the High Street behind you a new 'Food Hall' is being constructed, but it won't alter the character of the street at the end of which is Gresham's School, founded by the discoverer of That Law ('bad money drives out good', as he told Elizabeth I). Recent old boys: W. H. Auden and Benjamin Britten.

Norwich Cathedral

Although there are more townsmen than countrymen even in East Anglia, still popularly thought of as agricultural—and what beautiful towns have had to be left out of this book, like Eye, Beccles and Bungay!—you only have to look at the map to see how the roads all converge on this central city. A city is a place with a cathedral; and it is not mere coincidence that the only other place on the map showing a similar convergence is Thetford, which was the seat of the bishopric after the Conquest from 1075 to 1094.

But the Normans knew a good defensive site—a hill in the bend of a river, which you may find from Durham to Toledo on the Tagus—when they saw one. The Castle, with its squareness, its whiteness, and its tier upon tier of high rounded windows so reminiscent of London's White Tower, is on high ground in a bend of the River Wensum. It now houses an unrivalled collection of the works of (what else!) the Norwich School. It had something to do with the *light*, which, if you are driving up, you begin to see getting, well, one can only say brighter, once you pass Colchester. Hence Gainsborough and above all Constable, although they were not in the Norwich School, which was founded by Constable's contemporary (more or less; 1768-1821) John Crome ('Old Crome' since his son 'Young Crome' was also a painter) and John Sell Cotman.

From the castle's top you can see outlines of the old walled city (some of the wall is still there); but the cathedral, come upon from the south, is, like so many East Anglian glories, a surprise, a revelation. Behind this 1470 west window, is a nave of tremendous round Norman pillars surmounted by a much later, marvellous lierne vaulted roof. A good way to be shown round would be lying on a trolley with field glasses to see the unsurpassed roof bosses here and in the cloisters, the largest in England.

A snug city in open, often lonely, country, Norwich has thirty-three other medieval churches, the famous Maddermarket and Theatre Royal, a music festival since 1824, a colourful striped-canvas market next to glorious St Peter Mancroft, the perfect medieval Elm Hill, and Strangers Hall. To quote the poet Louis MacNeice

Sir Thomas Browne was right and so was Dame
(Or Mother or Lady) Julian to descry
That life, in spite of all, is a flame and a pure flame.
Norwich gave both a place in which to live and think,
And both gave Norwich back some ends
                    at which to aim…

From medieval mystic to shoes and insurance; quite a range, Norwich.

A Norfolk lane in spring

Hingham

You can only get to Hingham by minor roads, through cornlands dotted with woods, which makes its Georgian elegance all the more of a delightful surprise. Behind the viewer of this scene, there are more Georgian houses round a little triangular green with a hexagonal white-weatherboard bus pavilion ('shelter' seems too prosaic a word). Beyond the church is a much larger green with more of the same, often with Dutch gables clapped on the end. But people here were tough as well as elegant. In 1638 the Rev. Robert Peck was a co-founder of Hingham, Massachusetts, fleeing as a Puritan. The stone mounted into the bottom-right of the two-gabled building is a piece of granite sent in 1913 in return for the old mounting block sent from here in 1911. In 1637 Samuel Lincoln, who was born here, emigrated, and in the huge church (fourteenth-century with arches of unusual pinkish stone and a colossal flint tower) there is a bronze bust (no beard) of his descendant, Abraham. '...many citizens of the United States have erected this memorial in the hope that for all ages between that land and this land and all lands there shall be malice toward none and with charity for all'.

[47]

Blickling Hall

Blickling Hall is practically the Platonic Form, or the distillation of everybody's dream of the perfect Jacobean great house. You are looking at the south and *shorter* end of this huge oblong and behind the turret on your right, after you've ascended the superb staircase in the central hall, come the South Drawing Room, the Ante-Room and then the 123-foot Long Gallery with the best Jacobean ceiling in England. It is no place for a couple to visit of whom one likes classically landscaped gardens, with great rides and vistas with a Tuscan temple or a mausoleum at the end (in this case for the 2nd Earl of Buckingham, in 1762 Ambassador to St Petersburg), and the other likes marvellous furniture

and, perhaps most of all, moulded plaster ceilings. They would need separate tours—and still hardly touch on the history. This house was built in 1625 by the 1st Baronet Hobart. The 5th Bart. was made 1st Earl of Buckingham because his sister was, well, a friend of George II. The last owner before the National Trust was Lord Lothian, popular Ambassador to the United States who died in 1940. But previous houses here belonged to Sir T. Erpingham (who lent his cloak to Henry V for his incognito night tour of Agincourt camp), Sir J. Fastolf (whence Falstaff), Geoffrey Boleyn (great-grandfather of Anne)....

Caister Castle

Caister-on-Sea is now practically a Yarmouth suburb, an unremarkable collection of caravans and holiday camps. The word is of course simply an anglicisation of the Latin *castrum*, a camp. The Romans built their town here in about 125 A.D., complete with seamen's hostel and public baths: you can still see some of the remains. The town was a defence post (though the 'Count of the Saxon Shore' and his *foederati* forces became ever less Roman and more Saxon—the latter being fully established here by 400) and traded with the Rhineland, but the Romans were not exactly the first on the scene. In Norwich Castle Museum there are some Bronze Age (about 700 B.C.) cloak fasteners of *gold*, from Ireland, which were dug up here and show that the import-export business has a long history.

Caister Castle, a couple of miles inland, sounds tremendously Roman too, but in fact has nothing whatever to do with them. You realise when you see, from your country lane, over a ridge of cornland, the tower with its rather home-made-looking blue and yellow flag flying; you climb the ridge and come slightly *down* to it. *This* was a commanding Roman site lording it over the vast expanse of rich (now) cornland? Even though the whole geography was different then, with the shoreline further away? No. It was built by, or rather for, Sir John Fastolf (1378-1459) of whom there are conflicting reports—i.e. he served with distinction at Agincourt (1415), but after an English defeat at Patay was deprived of the Garter 'for cowardice'. Either way, he amassed a huge fortune (and his name, slightly altered, immortalised by Shakespeare) and left the castle, in a will disputed with much violence, to John Paston. The Paston Letters, the famous first great English correspondence, have everything from economic detail to love-letters.

It now seems to be next door to an intensive farm and has a motor museum in the middle of fields with 'the largest collection of motor vehicles in Great Britain from 1893 to the present time'.

Overy Staithe

Overy Staithe is reached by a road, 'to West Harbour' across which this building, once a grain store and now a chandlery, faces a row of sailing dinghies and a view across tough-grassed marshes and creeks to the eastern end of Scolt Head nature reserve. The road turns back again after a couple of hundred yards to the main road and its welcoming pub, The Hero. Everybody wears jeans and guernseys (children, too); all have that pale tan that looks so much healthier and weatherbeaten than the deepest-fried Mediterranean-brown. There is the constant obbligato of halyards slapped against masts by the wind. This is in one of seven parishes under the general aegis of Burnham Market, all containing the word Burnham. The hero was of course Nelson, born at Burnham Thorpe, although, says Henry Irving in *Tidal Havens of the Wash and Humber*, a real chandlery-type book, 'to judge from the Nelsonian bric-a-brac in the shops of Overy Staithe one would think that the Hero spent his youth breathing the salt air from the top of Gun Hill and cutting his sailing teeth in the treacherous white water of Burnham Harbour mouth ... but he was sent at a tender age to schools in Norwich and North Walsham ... Nelson's first feel of underfoot planking was at Chatham. If it had been at Burnham Overy he may have had second thoughts!'

The Bure near Ludham

Approaching Ludham from seaward, past signs pointing to such marvellous names as Oby and Trett's Loke, you seem to be able to see over distances far more majestic (and under infinitely greater skyscapes) than you would in whatever counties Noel Coward thought were less flat than Norfolk. It stands between the river Ant flowing south, the Bure east, and the Thurn also south (this time on the seaward side), but you have only to walk for a few minutes to water level, where sails pass through the trees. There is the usual superb church: this one has a 1493 painted screen over the chancel arch, with the arms of Queen Elizabeth on the other side all ready for a hasty substitution during the post-Mary reaction. Off to the right of this characteristic Broadland view are the ruins of Norfolk's oldest abbey, St Benet's Hulme, of which the Bishop of Norwich has been titular abbot since Henry VIII's time. As it is practically at the confluence of the Ant and the Bure he makes his visitation by water —much the easiest way to get from many an A to many a B round here.

Sandringham

The earliest known named owner of Sand(e)r(s)ingham, preceding one Cornish Henley by about 1200 years, was an Anglo-saxon called (probably) Deorsige. Sandringham was once identical with neighbouring Dersingham, the *ham* (village) of the people (*ing*) of Deorsige. The *Sand* came later. Henley (whose wife's family owned it for 100 years) built a Georgian house which he left in 1843 to Charles Spencer Cowper from whom Queen Victoria bought it in 1862 for her son, later Edward VII. He turned it into today's Victorian Jacobethan mansion.

We are here on the narrow estuarine 'Greensand Belt' widening down-wards from Hunstanton; a land for heath and pine. From walks in the public country park within its 20,100 acres you can see right across the Wash to the famous church tower, the Boston Stump in Lincolnshire. There is also a great deal of very efficient mixed farming, with crops from wheat to lavender—and pick-it-yourself fruit. Everywhere there is a tremendous impression of *space*; smooth lawns bordered by a marvel-lous woodland walk with, in summer, blazing shrubs under great firs. It is happy, too, with Christmas snow. The royal Christmas broadcast tradition began here with George V, who said 'Dear old Sandringham, the place I love better than anywhere else in the world'.

Burnham Overy Mill

This water-mill near Burnham Overy (which is on the River Burn and also near Overy Staithe), is on the road which runs along the North Norfolk coast from Hunstanton to Cromer, sometimes giving you a glimpse of the sea over marshes, then plunging through lovely sweeps of cornfield with often surprisingly large woods. Looking at it is very like the experience of being in some foreign museum gazing at something you love which also just happens to be famous (not that this mill is; such beautiful things are two a penny in East Anglia). You stand there in a trance, then, rumble rumble gabble gabble, a conducted party comes for a mini-lecture about it, and then leaves you to it again. Only here it is not conducted tours, but traffic. There is a lovely line of cottages, a private riverside garden and a narrow bridge under which mill-race-speed water tumbles, with a mysterious sign *6 Tons except Buses, Up To 7 Tons Any Axle*. Suddenly ten cars and a coach from North Wales roaringly follow two tractors (it is all farmland with lots of lovely real dung and cows). But you will be rewarded if you go on westwards to the nearest bit of verge where you can park. Then walk back, peer through dusty windows at bits of old machinery, and relish the silence of 160 years ago.

Heacham, lavender field

One of the saddest social casualties of World War II was the famous street cries of London. There are people not yet sixty who can remember not only the muffin man's but the most beautiful one, many think, of all—appropriately—the one for lavender.

> Won't you buy my sweet lavender
> Sixteen branches for a penny
> You buy it once, you buy it twice
> It makes your clothes smell sweet and nice.

Here, in July, there are rows of purple, head-swimming crops as though you were in Provence, not just a few miles north of King's Lynn (sandy soil and a lot of sun). Heacham has in Caley Mill the undisputed centre of English lavender production. They have about a hundred acres and have developed their own unique harvesting machine. They export hugely, having their own New York warehouse. One third of the crop is dried, for sachets, pot-pourris etc., and from the other two-thirds they distil the oil, the essential constituent of all lavender toiletries (150 tons gives 500 litres). A bush ends its useful life after five years, and there is constant experiment with new varieties which may take ten years to pass all the tests. The farm is now run by the Head family; it was started in 1932 by one Linn Chilvers, short for surely the most appropriate possible name—Linnaeus, the father of botanical classification.

Blakeney Marshes

In Blakeney Point—which is the spit of shingle and sand dunes sometimes rising to the, for here, vast height of eighty feet—the National Trust, which acquired it in 1912, has surely one of its most beautiful and, well, *unspoilt* territories. To walk along it you must go four miles east to Cley, where the River Glaven, seen here at Blakeney harbour, does one of those East Anglian right-angle turns just short of the sea, creating this paradise for natural life. There are thousands of terns and over 260 other species, wonderful flowers like Sea Campion, Yellow-horned Poppy and Tree Lupin—and what about a salt marsh in July with the Sea Lavender blooming! But you can get here by boat by the much shorter water route (and see seals basking on the way). The high posts are to save boats from being dashed to pieces on land in exceptional tides. 'So many birdwatchers descended on the village of Cley that they spent Saturday night sleeping in church porches, bus shelters, barns and on public house floors,' said the *Times* in late August 1985. They had come to see a reported whimbrel, a bird usually migrating only between Siberia and Japan. 'Ar', said the young man in the car park hut, 'that went to Salthouse yest'dy, but that's back here today; likes it here, I reckon.'

King's Lynn

King's Lynn is a classical reminder of the fact that before America was discovered (and ports grew in the west and south) and before the north saw the Industrial Revolution, *this* was the important coast. In the early fourteenth century Lynn was the third largest port in England. It was one of the few towns on the Royalist side in the Civil War—hence the smiling Charles II in a niche on the north wall of this enchanting Custom House, built 1683. But the great sights start much farther south

—well, five minutes' walk, down several little lanes from Queen (further up, King) Street to the Ouse with its sea horizon. The stupendous two-towered St Margaret's (Charles Burney once organist, Fanny Burney born here) and the Tudor merchant's house, Hampton Court, that 'just growed' to surround a lovely cobbled quad, face the Saturday Market. Then comes a lovely dark-red brick complex of Hanseatic 'stillyard' premises, then Clifton House, then Fermoy Centre (folk museum,

rehearsal rooms, restaurant, jolly drinks terrace overlooking Ouse and not only during brilliant high summer Festival). Then the vast beautiful square called Tuesday Market (and one on Friday too). Then 'Bishop's Lynn' with the 'chapel-of-ease' St Nicholas, (chapel? It holds the Philharmonia Orchestra and an audience). Once the spires and towers of this Norfolk Venice were sea-marks, now there are the silos and tank farms of a flourishing industrial port. There is the best of both worlds here.

Little Snoring

A little south of Walsingham, England's version of Lourdes with its famous pilgrimage-shrine to Mary, is Great Snoring with its rich-fanlighted Georgian houses round a neat green and lots of hanging flowers. A little further south, before more modest Little Snoring in its meadows, is this extraordinary church, right in the fields. Etymology soon disposes of any jokes about sleepiness, since it means 'Snear's people', he being some invader called, in fact, 'the Bright' or 'the Alert'. The round Saxon tower, predating the Norman church built on to it around 1100, is of flint because the further you go back the more the local absence of stone, even for corners, forced them to use local flint, and in those days you certainly needed a tower for a look-out. An electric fence actually goes right up to the marvellous porch, with a Norman arch, a Gothic one above that and a Saracenic one above *that*. The quiet, white little church contains windows of all periods, like a textbook—and its history does not stop with the Perpendicular (on the north side of the nave); a wall tablet records the RAF use of this church in the war; and here are two verses from a framed poem by an airman revisiting it:

I returned to Snoring airfield
The way was hard to find

For over paths and taxi-ways
Nature had thrown a blind
Of grass and twisted bramble
Willowherb and clinging vine
No longer there the Nissen huts
In which men slept and dined.

Deserted then the hangars stood,
Empty, broken, gaunt and grey
Only wheeling birds were there
To welcome me that day
And when some silent mystic hand
Rolled back the fleeting years
I saw this dead place filled with life
And my eyes were wet with tears . . .

Cromer

For an East Anglian sea town Cromer is a very up-and-down place—physically. It actually has cliffs on both sides. Its Perpendicular church, with the tallest tower in Norfolk, served as a seamark and lighthouse on these dangerous waters until the real lighthouse at Overstrand was built. It was in latish Victorian times that everything happened that changed Cromer from a crab-fishing village to a rather select resort (the excellent sandy beaches being just the thing). The railway arrived. In 1895 the vast Hotel de Paris, all dark red brick and copper-turreted towers and luxury, was built, overlooking the pier authorised a couple of years later. Edward VII became patron of the golf club....

But old traditions remained. Cromer crabs are still famous, and the skill obtained in the sturdy broad-beamed boats—and even more the courage—found national recognition in the best-known of all lifeboatmen, Henry Blogg (died 1954) who won the RNLI's Gold Medal three times *and* the George Cross. Like many other villages on this coast, Cromer is a survivor; the port of Shipden (of which it was a part) was swallowed by the sea back in the early 1400s. Other places lose their piers. Cromer's, with its 500-seat Pavilion, was the subject of a TV show about the decline of this form of live entertainment; its 1985 offering was extended to the end of August 'by popular demand'.

Great Snoring, the Old Rectory

Hortus conclusus, a walled garden, secret, enclosed; no wonder it is part of the marvellous sensuous imagery of the Song of Solomon. 'A garden enclosed is my sister, my spouse; a spring shut up, a fountain sealed. Thy plants are an orchard of pomegranates, with pleasant fruits; camphire, with spikenard, spikenard and saffron; calamus and cinnamon, with all trees of frankincense . . .'. The present occupants of Great Snoring Old Rectory (and before that it was a manor house) haven't got round to frankincense and pomegranates yet, having run it as a hotel for only eight years. From the replanted walled garden you can see the church, but only in winter when the trees are bare. It is all part of the English genius for creating Inner Space. Norfolk has a great tradition of fine church houses built on its large estates, and this is one of the oldest (1525) and finest.

Norfolk, winter